Quick & Easy Internet Activities for the One-Computer Classroom

Ancient Civilizations

by Edie Evans

20 Fun, Web-Based Activities
With Reproducible Graphic Organizers That Enable Kids to Research and Learn—On Their Own!

New York • Toronto • London • Auckland • Sydney
Mexico City • New Dehli • Hong Kong • Buenos Aires

In Loving
Memory of
Denis Audley Evans
(1923-2000)

Acknowledgments

Thanks to my editor, Maria Chang,
and my segosha, David Evans.

Scholastic Inc. grants teachers permission to photocopy the activity sheets from this book for classroom use. No other part of this publication may be reproduced in whole or in part, or stored in a retrieval system, or transmitted in any form or by any means, electronic, mechanical, photocopying, recording, or otherwise, without written permission of the publisher. For information regarding permission, write to Scholastic Inc., 557 Broadway, New York, NY 10012.

Cover design by **Norma Ortiz**
Interior design by **Holly Grundon**
Interior illustrations by **Delana Bettoli**

Cover image from "Pyramids, The Inside Story" at
www.pbs.org/wgbh/nova/pyramid
Copyright © 1997 WGBH Educational Foundation and PBS

ISBN: 0-439-28042-7
Copyright © 2002 by Edie Evans
All rights reserved.
Printed in the U.S.A.
1 2 3 4 5 6 7 8 9 10 40 09 08 07 06 05 04 03 02

Contents

Using This Book

Welcome to *Quick & Easy Internet Activities for the One-Computer Classroom: Ancient Civilizations*. The 20 Web-based activities in this book will expand your students' knowledge about a number of well-known and lesser-known ancient civilizations, while simultaneously building their writing, language, and Internet-research skills. The World Wide Web features a wealth of information that is constantly being added and updated, and is a perfect resource for learning about ancient civilizations. Students can go online to read the latest news as well as access the most recent links at the touch of a button.

What's Inside

This book is divided into five chapters, by worldwide geography: Africa, Mesopotamia, Asia, Europe and the Mediterranean, and the Americas. Each of the 20 activities in this book is accompanied by a teacher page with background information, step-by-step mini-lesson, and extension activity. Reproducible student pages provide students with simple directions, graphic organizers, and recording space to help them with their online research. On page 6, you'll find a listing of the World History Standards that the activities meet. You'll also find a reproducible assessment sheet that you can use to evaluate students' projects on page 7.

Accessing the Web Sites

In the fast-paced world of the Internet, Web sites can come and go quickly. In addition, some URLs (Uniform Resource Locations, or Web site addresses) are so long, students can accidentally type in the wrong address. For these reasons, we decided to publish all the necessary URLs on our own Web site.

To access the Web sites for the activities in this book, go to:

http://www.scholastic.com/profbooks/netexplorations/index.htm

This address also appears at the top of the teacher and student pages. Click on the book cover for *Ancient Civilizations*. Then, click on the links under each activity name to access the appropriate Web sites needed to complete the activity. Remember to bookmark this site or add it to your favorites.

NOTE: You may still want to check out the Web sites yourself before using them in your classroom. By familiarizing yourself with their content, you'll be able to help students navigate through them more efficiently.

Tips for Managing Web-based Activities

The activities in this book require students to spend some time on the computer to do research and complete at least a portion of their worksheets. Whether you have only one computer in your classroom or have access to a computer lab, here are some tips for helping students manage limited time on the computer effectively:

★ Assign each student or small group about 15 minutes of computer time in rotation. (Most of the activities in this book can be done by students in small groups.) Have the rest of the class complete the non-computer part of the activity, or give them related activities to do while waiting for their turn at the computer.

★ Before students go to the computer, have them read their worksheets carefully so they have a clear, focused idea of what to look for. When they go online, tell students that they don't need to read everything on a site—they can just browse for the information they need and then jot it down on their worksheets.

★ You can hook up your computer to a video monitor or a projector, and have your whole class browse the Web together. Students can participate by taking turns clicking the hyperlinks or reading the information aloud.

★ If you don't have online capabilities in your classroom, try offline software, such as Web Whacker (www.bluesquirrel.com), to capture all the pages in a Web site and download them. Students can then view the Web site from computers that aren't connected to the Internet. You can also save Web pages as viewable documents and/or print them out, but they will most likely not include pictures and graphics.

More Tips for Smooth Surfing

★ Review with students the basics of using their Internet browsers, such as typing in exact URLs, scrolling, going back and forward between Web pages, using hyperlinks, printing, and copying and pasting images.

★ Consider creating "Browser Basics" help sheets or index cards, and post them near the computer.

★ Many Web sites can contain an overwhelming barrage of information. Encourage students to "browse" the Web sites for the information they need, and not worry about reading everything.

World History Standards

The information and lessons featured in this book meet the following World History Standards:

ERA 2:
Early Civilizations and the Emergence of Pastoral Peoples, 4000–1000 BCE

Standard 1: The major characteristics of civilization and how civilizations emerged in Mesopotamia, Egypt, and the Indus Valley

Standard 2: How agrarian societies spread and new states emerged in the third and second millennia BCE

Standard 3: The political, social, and cultural consequences of population movements and militarization in Eurasia in the second millennium BCE

Standard 4: Major trends in Eurasia and Africa from 4000-1000 BCE

ERA 3:
Classical Traditions, Major Religions, and Giant Empires, 1000 BCE-300 CE

Standard 1: Innovation and change from 1000-600 BCE: horses, ships, iron, and monotheistic faith

Standard 2: The emergence of Aegean civilization and how interrelations developed among peoples of the eastern Mediterranean and Southwest Asia, 500-200 BCE

Standard 3: How major religions and large-scale empires arose in the Mediterranean basin, China, and India, 500 BCE-300 CE

ERA 4:
Expanding Zones of Exchange and Encounter, 300–1000 CE

Standard 6: The rise of centers of civilization in Mesoamerica and Andean South America in the first millennium CE

ERA 5:
Intensified Hemispheric Interactions, 1000–1500 CE

Standard 6: The expansion of states and civilizations in the Americas, 1000-1500 CE

ERA 6:
The Emergence of the First Global Age, 1450–1770

Standard 1: How the transoceanic interlinking of all major regions of the world from 1450–1600 CE led to global transformations

Source: National Center for History in the Schools

Project Evaluation Form

NAME: ______________________________ **DATE:** ______________

PROJECT: ____

Criteria	Score				
	Poor				Excellent
Follows Directions	1	2	3	4	5
Collaborates With Other Students *(cooperation, flexibility)*	1	2	3	4	5
Uses Computer Time Effectively *(goal-oriented, navigation skills)*	1	2	3	4	5
Curriculum Content *(research, organization, creativity)*	1	2	3	4	5
Writing *(clarity, organization, spelling, grammar)*	1	2	3	4	5
Supporting Visuals *(if applicable)*	1	2	3	4	5

TOTAL SCORE ______________

Comments:

____

____

____

____

GO TO: www.scholastic.com/profbooks/netexplorations/index.htm

Social Studies

Egyptian Kingdoms

Students record the major advances and events that occurred during the Early- to Late-Dynastic periods of ancient Egypt (3000–332 BC).

BACKGROUND

The ancient Egyptians invented a writing system (hieroglyphics), built extraordinary pieces of architecture (the pyramids, ancient temples), and developed a complex, highly structured government. The history of ancient Egypt is divided into periods in which different dynasties ruled, each of which is marked by various cultural, technological, and historic advances.

DOING THE ACTIVITY

1. Engage students in a discussion about ancient Egypt. Ask them, What are some of the things that come to mind when you think of ancient Egypt? *(Pyramids, pharaohs, mummies, etc.)*
2. Explain that most civilizations have histories that are divided into distinct time periods that are usually significant for a number of reasons, such as a famous ruler, a war, a natural disaster, or a profound technological or cultural advancement.
3. Photocopy and distribute page 9 to each student or student pair that will be working at a computer.
4. Have students click on the links at the above Web site and do research to complete the chart on their sheet.

More To Do:

Time Line of Ancient Egypt

Challenge students to create a bulletin board display showing the history of ancient Egypt. Divide students into seven groups and assign each group one of the eras from the chart. Have each group compile the information collected by students for their era, then choose the events they want to feature for their section of the display. Encourage students to include captioned pictures or drawings.

Name(s) ____________________________________

GO TO: www.scholastic.com/profbooks/netexplorations/index.htm

The Egyptian Kingdoms

Ancient Egypt flourished for many centuries. Click on the links at the above Web site to learn about the history of ancient Egypt. Record at least two things that are significant about each of the time periods below.

Era	Significant Events
Early Dynastic (approx. time period: ______________)	
Old Kingdom (approx. time period: ______________)	
1st Intermediate (approx. time period: ______________)	
Middle Kingdom (approx. time period: ______________)	
2nd Intermediate (approx. time period: ______________)	
New Kingdom (approx. time period: ______________)	
Late Dynastic (approx. time period: ______________)	

GO TO: www.scholastic.com/profbooks/netexplorations/index.htm

Social Studies
Language Arts
Art

Egyptian Burial Customs

Students explore the connection between pyramids, hieroglyphics, and mummies, and create a brochure for an imaginary Egyptian tomb.

BACKGROUND

Funeral rites were one of the most important customs in ancient Egypt. Not only were the dead preserved as mummies, they were also buried with food, personal possessions, and tools in preparation for their trip to the afterlife. Tomb walls were decorated with art and hieroglyphs describing daily life, as well as what those who were buried hoped to find after death. Pyramids were built, in part, as burial chambers for the pharaohs—a place for them to pass safely into the afterlife.

DOING THE ACTIVITY

1. Hold a class discussion about the Egyptian concept of burial and the afterlife. Ask students what they know about mummies, pyramids, and hieroglyphics. Make a list of movies, books, and games students know that incorporate these elements of Egyptian culture.

2. Photocopy and distribute page 11 to each student pair or small group.

3. Invite students to explore the links at the above Web site to help them fill out the brochure. If students are working in pairs or small groups, encourage them to divide the work so that each student works on one section of the brochure.

4. When students have finished, invite them to share their brochures with the class. Ask them to summarize what they've learned about burial customs in ancient Egypt. In what ways were the Egyptians' funeral customs similar to or different from our own?

More To Do:

Mummy Museum

Invite your class to create a "mummy museum," displaying student-created artifacts "gathered" from Egyptian expeditions. Students could display their brochures next to their artifacts to show where their pieces came from.

Name(s) ____

GO TO: www.scholastic.com/profbooks/netexplorations/index.htm

Tombs of Egypt

Explore the links at the above Web site to learn about Egyptian tombs. Then create a tour brochure of the inside of an imaginary tomb. If possible, decorate the brochure with pictures you downloaded from the Web sites.

History *of the* **Tomb**

This tomb is called

________________.

It is located at

________________.

____

is buried here. This is his/her history:

____

____

____

____

Map *of the* **Tomb**

Draw a map here of the tomb.

What's Inside

Here are some items you will find in this tomb:

- ________________
- ________________
- ________________
- ________________
- ________________
- ________________
- ________________
- ________________

GO TO: www.scholastic.com/profbooks/netexplorations/index.htm

Social Studies
Geography
Critical Thinking

Egypt & Nubia

Students compare the neighboring kingdoms of Egypt and Nubia, and explore the relationship between the two kingdoms.

BACKGROUND

The ancient land of Nubia was located in the African desert just south of Egypt and divided by the Nile River. Nubia was rich in gold, ivory, ebony, and other resources, and became a trade center for central Africa. Sometime between 1950 BC and 1000 BC, parts of Nubia fell under Egyptian rule. During this time, Nubians adopted some of Egypt's customs and culture. When rivaling states began to tear Egypt apart around 750 BC, Nubia seized the opportunity by invading Egypt. Nubian pharaohs ruled over a unified Egyptian and Nubian state for about 60 years.

DOING THE ACTIVITY

1. If possible, show students a map of Nubia. (Click on the links at the above Web site to view or download a map.) Point out that Nubia was located along the Nile River, just south of Egypt. As neighboring kingdoms, Egypt and Nubia were similar in many ways. In fact, Nubians adopted some of Egypt's customs and culture.

2. Photocopy and distribute page 13 to each student. Invite students to learn more about Nubia and Egypt by exploring the links at the above Web site.

3. Have students write things about Egypt and Nubia in their respective circles of the Venn diagram. In the overlapping area, ask students to write things both kingdoms had in common.

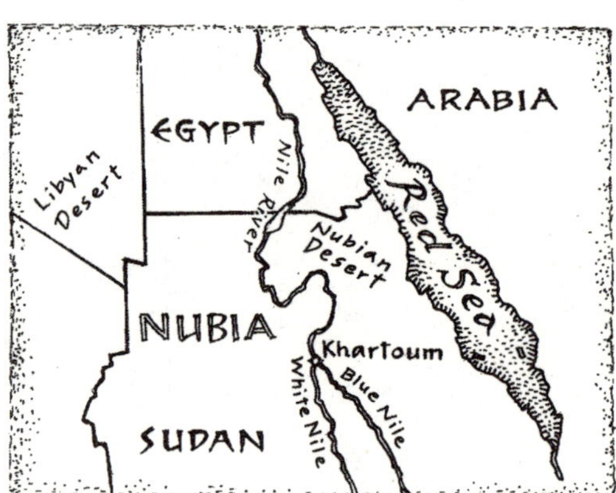

More To Do:

Neighboring Nations

Pair up students and have them research two modern-day neighboring nations. Ask them to describe the relationship between the two countries. For example, they may research the United States and Canada. Ask, Do the two countries have anything in common? If so, what are they? How are they different? Do the two nations get along? Why or why not? Invite each pair to present their findings to the class.

Name(s) ____

GO TO: www.scholastic.com/profbooks/netexplorations/index.htm

Neighbors on the Nile

The neighboring kingdoms of Egypt and Nubia had an uneasy relationship. At one point, Egypt invaded Nubia. Centuries later, the tables were turned when Nubian pharaohs conquered and ruled over Egypt. Explore the links at the above Web site to learn more about both kingdoms. Fill in the Venn diagram below to compare these two powerful civilizations.

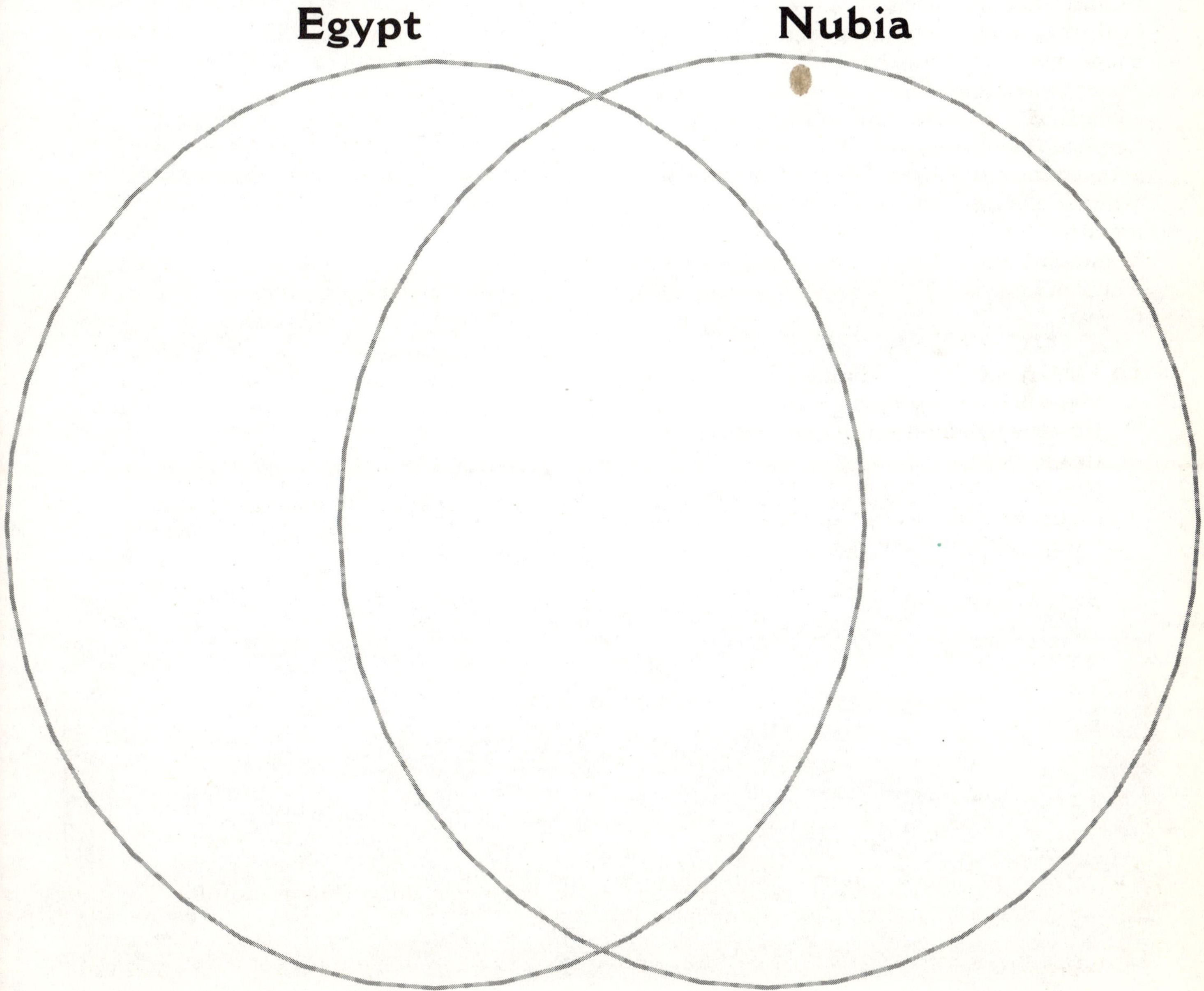

GO TO: www.scholastic.com/profbooks/netexplorations/index.htm

Social Studies

The History of Nubia

Students do research on the Web to fill in missing information about the ancient kingdom of Nubia.

BACKGROUND

Some experts believe Nubia was the first African civilization, flourishing even before Egypt. At one point in history, Nubia stretched over 1,000 miles along the Nile River from the middle of modern-day Sudan to southern Egypt. Nubia's geographic borders greatly varied over the years, causing each period of its history to have a unique culture with different rulers. Overview Nubian history with students to help them understand the difference between the various eras, the many rulers, and the changing borders of Nubia.

DOING THE ACTIVITY

1. Photocopy and distribute page 15 to each student, and inform them that they will be learning about the history of Nubia and its rulers.

2. Have students click on the links at the above Web site to fill in the blanks about the history of Nubia. Encourage students to note which Web site(s) they used to help them complete the article.

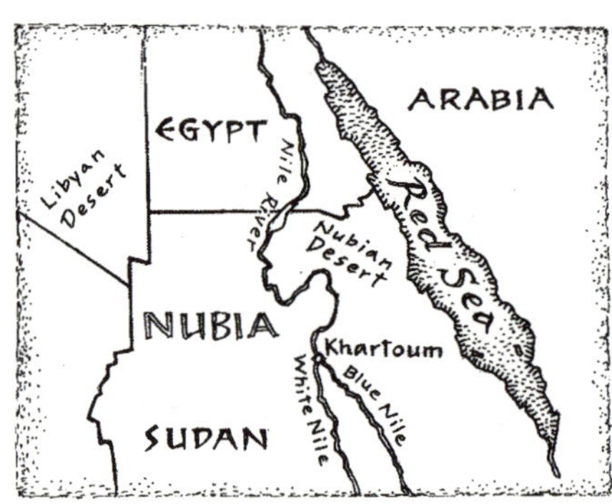

3. Once students have filled in all the blanks, you may want to discuss definitions of each word with them.

ANSWERS

Africa; Trade; A Group; C Group; Kerma; Egyptians; hieroglyphic; Piye; Napata; Dynasty; Assyrian; Meroitic

More To Do:

Modern-Day Nubia

The land that was called Nubia is now buried under the floodwaters of the Aswan Dam. Invite students to research the construction of the Aswan Dam and find out what happened to the Nubians that lived in the area that has since been flooded. Divide students into two groups—one of engineers, and the other of area residents. Have each group present arguments for or against the dam's construction.

Name(s) ____

GO TO: www.scholastic.com/profbooks/netexplorations/index.htm

In the Days of Nubia

Click on the links at the above Web site to help you fill in the blanks about the ancient kingdom of Nubia. Choose the correct words from the word bank below.

Word Bank			
	Kerma	Hieroglyphic	Meroitic
	Assyrian	Piye	Trade
	Africa	C Group	Dynasty
	Napata	A Group	Egyptians

The ancient land of Nubia was located in the continent of ________________, in what is now southern Egypt and northern Sudan. ________________ was an important part of Nubian society because the region was rich in valuable resources such as gold, incense, and ivory, which were exchanged for other goods.

An early kingdom, referred to as the ________________ by archaeologists, existed around 3900–2900 BC in the Lower Nile area. From 2500–1500 BC, a second kingdom, called the ________________, occupied the area known as Lower Nubia. At the same time in Upper Nubia, the ________________ culture thrived. The Kerma kings eventually extended their control to Lower Nubia. The ________________ colonized and ruled Nubia from about 1550–1100 BC. During this time, the Nubians worshipped Egyptian gods and used ________________ writing.

In 730 BC, a famous pharaoh from Kush named ________________ traveled north from his capital of ________________ to provide military protection to the Egyptian people of Thebes. He became ruler and founded Egypt's 25th ________________. This era ended when the ________________ army invaded the region in 663 BC, and the Nubians returned to Napata. By 295 BC, Nubia entered the ________________ period, named after its capital city of Meroe. This new capital was a great city complete with palaces, temples, shrines, and an observatory. This phase of Nubian history lasted until about 320 AD.

GO TO: www.scholastic.com/profbooks/netexplorations/index.htm

Social Studies Geography

The Fertile Crescent

Students familiarize themselves with the geography of Mesopotamia by completing a map.

BACKGROUND

In the Greek language, the word "Mesopotamia" means "the land between two rivers." Located in the highly arable land between the Tigris and the Euphrates rivers, Mesopotamia is also known as the Fertile Crescent. Mesopotamia covers the area that is now in eastern Syria, southeastern Turkey, and most of Iraq. Some of the earliest-known civilizations flourished in this region. The first cities were built in Mesopotamia and the first writing system was developed there. Although Mesopotamia was dominated by different groups throughout its history, this chapter will focus on the times that the Sumerians, Babylonians, and Assyrians ruled the area.

DOING THE ACTIVITY

1. Photocopy and distribute page 17 to each student. Inform students that Mesopotamia, a map of which is shown on their activity sheet, is considered by many to be the birthplace of civilization.

2. Encourage students to explore the links at the above Web site to familiarize themselves with the region. As they browse through the links, they should be able to find out the different areas in and around Mesopotamia. Have students label the areas that are numbered on their map.

3. Invite students to color their maps when they're finished.

ANSWERS

1. Assyria
2. Tigris River
3. Euphrates River
4. Sumer
5. Babylon
6. Ur
7. Persian Gulf
8. Arabian Desert
9. Red Sea
10. Jerusalem
11. Nile River
12. Sahara Desert
13. Mediterranean Sea

More To Do:

Class Map

You may want to recreate an enlarged version of the map of Mesopotamia to display on your wall or bulletin board. Invite students to help label and decorate the map with things they've learned about Mesopotamia.

Name(s) ____

GO TO: www.scholastic.com/profbooks/netexplorations/index.htm

Mapping Mesopotamia

Mesopotamia was located between the Tigris and Euphrates Rivers in what is now known as Iraq. Explore the links at the above Web site to identify and label the numbered areas on the map below. Each number represents a natural geographical site (such as a body of water or desert), a city, or a region.

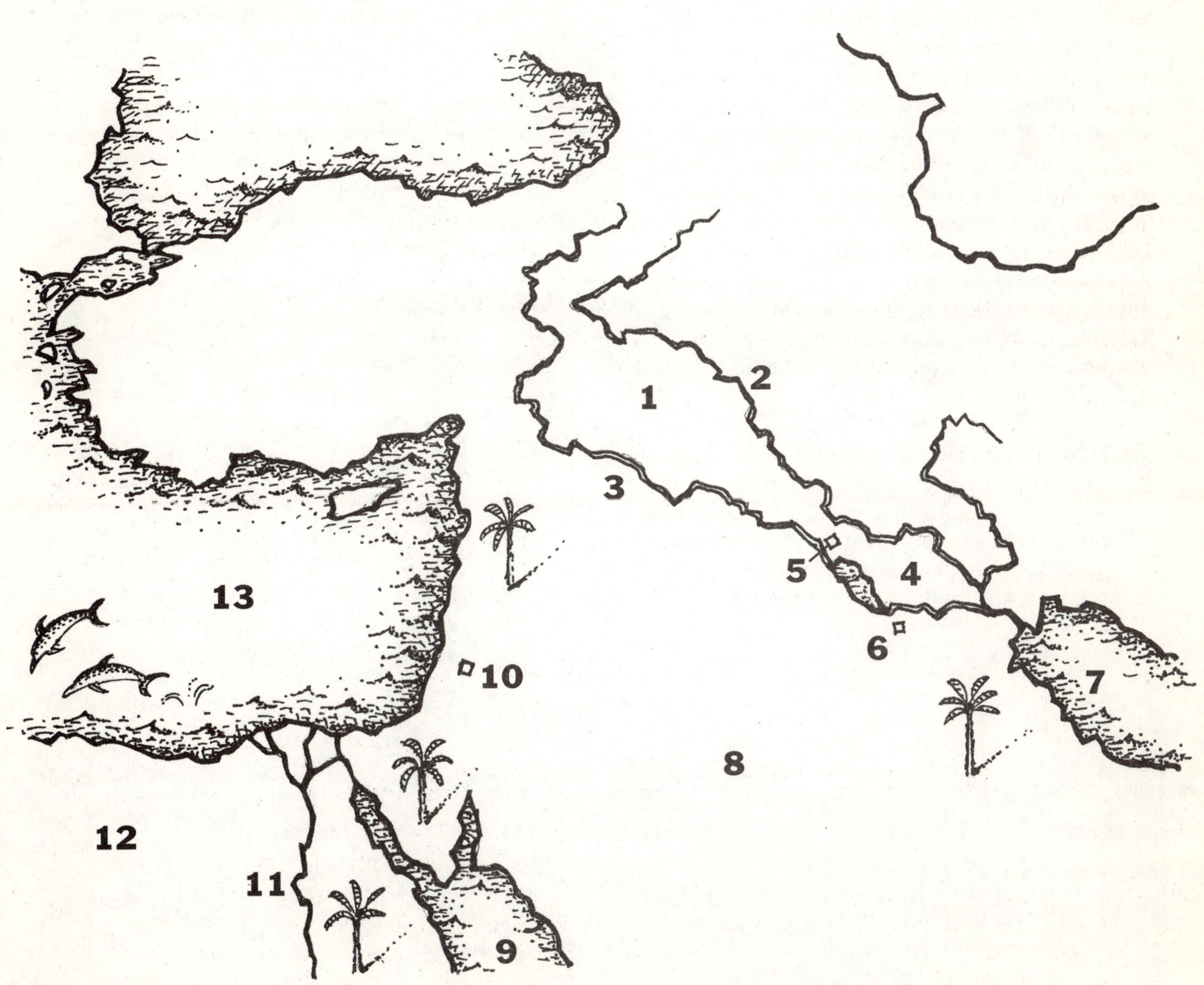

GO TO: www.scholastic.com/profbooks/netexplorations/index.htm

Social Studies Math

The Sumerians

Students learn about the Sumerians and their written language, called cuneiform. Then they use cuneiform numbers to complete math problems.

BACKGROUND

Sumer, in southern Mesopotamia, is the location of one of the world's earliest-known civilizations. The civilization began around 3500 BC and prospered until 2000 BC. The Sumerians were the first people to build magnificent cities, which later formed into city-states (or nations the size of cities). They also developed the first system of writing called *cuneiform*, which used pictograms or symbols to convey ideas. The Sumerians used pointed reeds to write on wet clay tablets, which were then baked to harden them. The word "cuneiform" comes from the Latin word *cuneus*, meaning *wedge*, since the symbols were generally wedge shaped.

DOING THE ACTIVITY

1. Hold a discussion about different ways to represent numbers. For example, the number 4 can be represented by writing the numeral 4, the word "four," or by drawing four lines. Explain that different cultures, both ancient and modern, have different ways of showing the same number.

2. Have students click on the links at the above Web site to learn about the Sumerians and their cuneiform number system.

3. Photocopy and distribute page 19 to each student. Challenge students to complete the basic math problems. Then have them draw the correct cuneiform numeral for their answer, referring to the key at the bottom of the page.

ANSWERS

1. 1
2. 40
3. 30
4. 16
5. 17
6. 13
7. 2
8. 3
9. 20
10. 11
11. 4
12. 50

More To Do:

New Age Numbers

Have students research other ways numbers are represented in different cultures. For example, students may want to look at Roman, Chinese, Arabic, and other numeral systems. Invite them to create a display showing the numbers 1 to 10 from each culture. You may then want to encourage students to invent a new way of writing numbers. Have them explain why they designed each number the way they did.

Name(s) ____

GO TO: www.scholastic.com/profbooks/netexplorations/index.htm

Sumerian Math

The Sumerians, the oldest known civilization in the world, developed an elaborate numbering system. Click on the links at the above Web site to learn more about cuneiform numbers. Then use the cuneiform numeral key below to solve these basic math problems.

1. ________ **+ 18 = 19**	**7.** **18 = 9 x** ________
2. ________ **= 50 – 10**	**8.** **15 ÷** ________ **= 5**
3. **5 x 6 =** ________	**9.** ________ **= 12 + 8**
4. ________ **÷ 4 = 4**	**10.** **17 –** ________ **= 6**
5. **14 + 3 =** ________	**11.** **10 x** ________ **= 40**
6. ________ **– 7 = 6**	**12.** ________ **÷ 5 = 10**

Cuneiform Numerals Key

1 𒁹	6	11	16	30
2	7	12	17	40
3	8	13	18	50
4	9	14	19	
5	10	15	20	

GO TO: www.scholastic.com/profbooks/netexplorations/index.htm

Social Studies
Language Arts

The Babylonians

Students learn about some famous sites of ancient Babylon and write a tour-guide script about the city.

BACKGROUND

Babylon started out as one of several small kingdoms in Mesopotamia. But under the rule of Hammurabi, from 1792 to 1750 BC, Babylon conquered nearby kingdoms and turned into a large empire. The Babylonians composed the first written code of laws, had sophisticated irrigation systems, and traded vigorously. After Hammurabi's death, Babylon lost most of its territory. But the city was magnificently rebuilt during the reign of Nebuchadnezzar II from 605 to 562 BC. The grand Ishtar Gate and the Hanging Gardens of Babylon were among its most famous sites.

DOING THE ACTIVITY

1. Find out what students know about ancient Babylon. Ask if they've ever heard of the Hanging Gardens of Babylon. Explain that the Hanging Gardens have been called one of the Seven Wonders of the Ancient World.
2. Photocopy and distribute page 21 to each student pair or small group.
3. Invite students to explore the links at the above Web site to learn more about some of the famous places in Babylon. Have them fill in their charts, then write a tour-guide script about the city of Babylon and its famous sites.

More To Do:

Travel Brochure for Babylon

Invite students to put together a travel brochure for the city of Babylon. If possible, have them download or draw pictures of famous places in the city. Then have them write descriptions of each site. They can even create an itinerary for tourists visiting the city.

Name(s) ____

GO TO: www.scholastic.com/profbooks/netexplorations/index.htm

The Wonders of Babylon

Click the links at the above Web site to explore the great city of Babylon and visit its famous sites. Fill in the chart below with information about each site. Then write a tour-guide script on the back of this page about the city and places to visit.

Places to Visit	Where is it?	Why is it famous?
Hanging Gardens		
Ishtar Gate		
Tower of Babel		
Temple of Marduk		

GO TO: www.scholastic.com/profbooks/netexplorations/index.htm

The Assyrians

Students complete a sequence chain diagram of the history of the Assyrians.

BACKGROUND

Known for being intimidating and forceful, the Assyrians ruled Mesopotamia with superior military prowess using iron weapons and horse-drawn chariots to conquer the land. They also introduced advancements such as postal delivery, paved roads, and invented the tumbler lock-and-key system. In 612 BC their capital of Ninevah was destroyed, ending Assyrian rule in Mesopotamia.

DOING THE ACTIVITY

1. Discuss different ways civilizations have gained power. Certain cultures became dominant as earlier ones became obsolete, or as natural geographical changes occurred. Some people, like the Assyrians, conquered other peoples and ruled by force.

2. Photocopy and distribute page 23 to each student pair or small group.

3. Have students browse the links at the above Web site to read about the history of the Assyrians. Then, have students complete the graphic organizer.

ANSWERS

746-727 BC: Tiglath-Pileser III conquers Syria and Israel, and becomes king of Babylonia; **721-705 BC:** Sargon II extends the Assyrian empire, deports the population of Israel, and divides Assyria into 70 provinces; **705-681 BC:** King Sennacherib destroys Babylon and makes Nineveh capital of Assyria; **681-669 BC:** King Esarhaddon rebuilds Babylon and captures Memphis (the capital of Egypt); **669-626 BC:** During King Ashurbanipal's reign, a revolution weakens Assyria's power; **612 BC:** The Medes and the Babylonians conquer the capital of Nineveh, ending the rule of the Assyrian Empire

More To Do:

A Show of Force

The Assyrians used their superior military skills to conquer neighboring kingdoms in Mesopotamia. Have students research Assyrian weaponry and military tactics and prepare a presentation about how they rose to power.

Name(s) ____

GO TO: www.scholastic.com/profbooks/netexplorations/index.htm

Forceful Rulers

In the chain-of-events graphic organizer below, each box lists a significant period and ruler in Assyrian history. Find out what important events occurred during each period by browsing on the links at the above Web site. Fill the boxes with information you find.

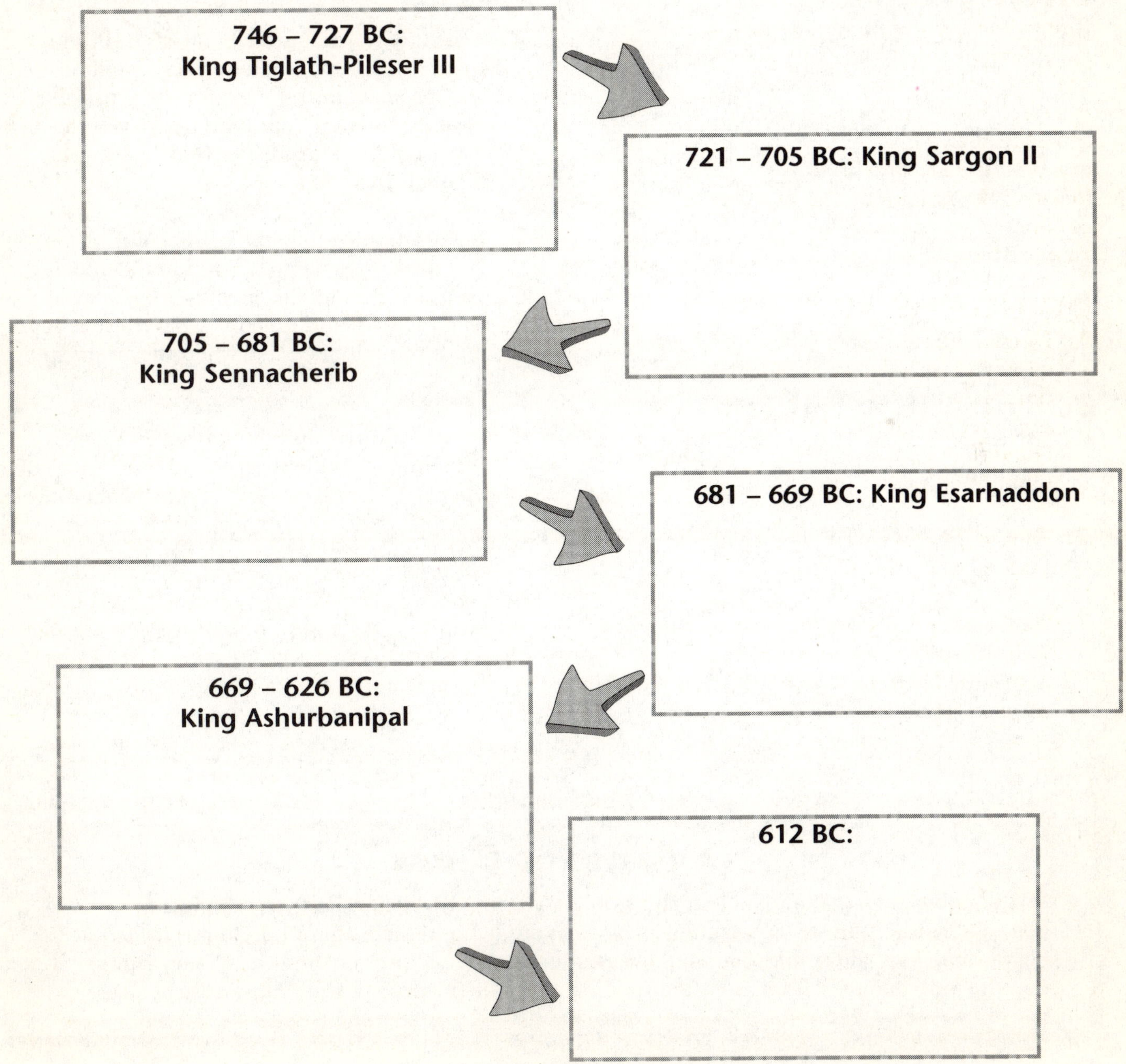

GO TO: www.scholastic.com/profbooks/netexplorations/index.htm

Social Studies
Geography
Language Arts

The Indus Valley

Students explore the ruins of the city of Harappa in the Indus Valley and sketch out a map.

BACKGROUND

Although much of the Indus Valley civilization remains a mystery, new discoveries are constantly being made. Around 2500 BC, the farming and herding communities centered in the river plains of present-day Pakistan and northwestern India began to unite. These new communities started planning and building cities. They developed a system of weights and measures, and used pictographs for writing. Because of changing river patterns, the Indus Valley civilization gradually dissolved into smaller settlements by around 1700 BC.

DOING THE ACTIVITY

1. Ask students, How do you think modern-day archaeologists find out about ancient civilizations? *(They may come across ruins of old cities or find artifacts that showed signs of civilization.)* What can they tell about an ancient civilization from their findings? *(How the people lived, what they did for fun or for work, etc.)*

2. Tell students that archaeologists didn't know that Harappa, an ancient city, existed in the Indus Valley until the 1920s, when they discovered its ruins. They are now trying to learn more about this ancient civilization through their findings.

3. Invite students to explore the ruins of Harappa by visiting the links at the above Web site. Encourage them to look at available pictures and imagine what those ruins might have looked like when they were still intact.

4. Photocopy and distribute page 25 to each student. Ask students to sketch out a map of the city of Harappa based on its ruins. Have them label different places, such as homes, baths, granaries, and more. On the back of the page, have students write a short story about life in Harappa. Ask, What do you think people did back then? Where did they go in the city, and why?

More To Do:

Digging for Clues

When archaeologists find ancient ruins, they have to rely on clues to learn about the people that lived there. For example, they may study the remains of old buildings to figure out what they were used for. Have students study pictures of the Indus Valley ruins on the Web and search for clues that might reveal the purpose of the different structures.

Name(s) ____

GO TO: www.scholastic.com/profbooks/netexplorations/index.htm

Lost City of Harappa

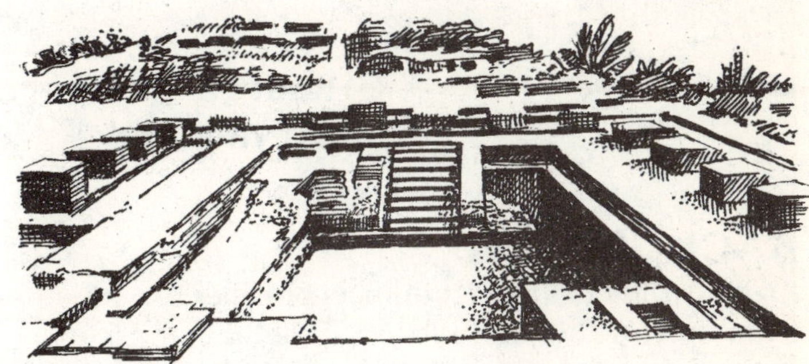

Explore the ruins around the Indus Valley by visiting the links at the above Web site. Below, sketch out a map of what you think the city of Harappa might have looked like 4,500 years ago. Label the different places in your map. On the back of this page, write about life in Harappa. What do you think people did back then? Where did they go? For what purpose?

GO TO: www.scholastic.com/profbooks/netexplorations/index.htm

Social Studies
Critical Thinking

The Vedic Age

Students compare and contrast the Aryan and Harappan cultures.

BACKGROUND

Around 1500 BC, large numbers of tribes from Iran and southern Russia called the Aryans migrated to India. They entered via the Khyber Pass in the Hindu Kush mountain range (in present-day Afghanistan and Pakistan). Although the Aryans originally mingled with the local people, their introduction of horses and creation of a powerful cavalry allowed them to conquer and rule many regions. This time in Indian history is known as the Vedic Age, named after the four Vedas—religious and philosophical hymns composed by the Aryans that laid the foundation for Hinduism.

DOING THE ACTIVITY

1. Discuss with students what it means to compare and contrast—to look for similarities and differences that exist between two elements or, in this case, two different cultures.

2. Tell students that they will be learning about another group of people, called the Aryans, who inhabited the Indus Valley around 1500 BC. Inform them that they will be comparing the Harappans' way of life with that of the Aryans.

3. Photocopy and distribute page 27 to each student pair or small group. Let students browse the links at the above Web site to read about the Harappans and the Aryans. Have them use the information they find on the Web sites to complete the chart.

4. Draw a large version of the chart on the board or on chart paper. Invite students to share their answers and compile them on the large chart. Then discuss the class's findings.

More To Do:

Religions of the World

The Vedas are the oldest sacred books of Hinduism, which is also one of the oldest religions in our world. Invite students to learn more about this religion and its teachings. Then compare Hinduism with other religions that exist today. How are they similar? How are they different?

Name(s) ____

GO TO: www.scholastic.com/profbooks/netexplorations/index.htm

The Harappans Meet the Aryans

Use the chart below to compare and contrast the Aryan culture with the Harappan culture. Browse the links at the above Web site to complete the chart.

	Harappans	Aryans
Time Period		
Type of Society		
Building of Cities		
Writing		
Social Organization		
Housing		
Clothing		
Use of Animals		
Transportation		

GO TO: www.scholastic.com/profbooks/netexplorations/index.htm

China's Ancient Dynasties

Students learn about three ancient Chinese dynasties and fill out a chart about them.

BACKGROUND

The Xia (2000–1500 BC), Shang (1700–1027 BC), and Zhou or Chou (1100–256 BC) dynasties are the basis of Chinese civilization. Until recent discoveries proved otherwise, the Xia were once considered a mythical culture. Still, little is known about them. It is known, however, that pottery and silk were already in existence by the time the Shang dynasty arrived. The Shang dynasty produced splendid bronze work and oracle bone writing. The Zhou dynasty founded the Iron Age in China, and introduced important schools of philosophy.

DOING THE ACTIVITY

1. Ask students, What is a dynasty? *(A line of rulers who belong to the same family)* Explain that in ancient China, a royal family would rule for hundreds of years until they were overthrown by a new family which took control.

2. Photocopy and distribute page 29 to each student pair or small group. Have students browse the links at the above Web site to fill in the chart with information about each of the three ancient dynasties.

3. Invite students to pick one of the dynasties and give an oral presentation about it.

ANSWERS

	Xia Dynasty	Shang Dynasty	Zhou (Chou) Dynasty
When did they rule?	2200-1750 BC (years may vary, depending on the Web site)	1750-1040 BC (years may vary, depending on the Web site)	1100-256 BC (years may vary, depending on the Web site)
How did they come to power?	unknown	People overthrew the last Xia ruler, who was a tyrant.	Ruler of the Chou (or Zhou) kingdom killed the ruler of the Shang dynasty.
What were some of their religious beliefs?	Rulers communicated with spirits for help and guidance.	Worshipped many gods and prayed to their ancestors. They also believed in human sacrifice.	Believed that the rulers were given power by the gods to rule. They also prayed to T'ien and to their ancestors, as well as to local nature gods.
What are some other interesting facts?	Answers may vary, but could include that they are well-known for their black-lacquered pottery.	Answers may vary, but could include that they developed a system of writing and were advanced in bronze metallurgy.	Answers may vary, but could include that during this time various schools of philosophy came into being, including Confucianism, Taoism, and Legalism.

More To Do:

Passing Down the Rule

Monarchies are like dynasties in that the right to rule is passed down from generation to generation within a royal family. Today, many monarchies are considered symbols of a country's unity—with the real power held by elected officials. Have students find out which countries today are still ruled by a monarchy. Then divide the class into two groups: Have each group debate about the advantages and disadvantages of being governed by a monarchy.

Name(s) ____________________

GO TO: www.scholastic.com/profbooks/netexplorations/index.htm

China's Ancient Dynasties

Learn about the three ancient Chinese dynasties listed below by clicking on the links at the above Web site. Fill in the chart with your findings. Then give an oral presentation to your class about one of the dynasties.

	Xia Dynasty	Shang Dynasty	Zhou (Chou) Dynasty
When did they rule?			
How did they come to power?			
What were some of their religious beliefs?			
What are some other interesting facts?			

GO TO: www.scholastic.com/profbooks/netexplorations/index.htm

The Chinese Art of Writing

Students learn about Chinese characters, then create their own characters.

BACKGROUND

The earliest examples of Chinese writing were called *oracle bones.* Existing from the time of the Shang dynasty, oracle bones were animal bones or turtle shells inscribed with characters that were used for divination (to foresee the future). The oracle bones became records of events during the Shang dynasty. The Zhou dynasty that followed produced early forms of calligraphy that were inscribed in bronze, carved in bamboo, and written on silk.

DOING THE ACTIVITY

1. Ask students, Why do you think writing is important in a society? *(It's a means of communication, of recording important events, etc.)* Have students think about how our alphabet differs from Chinese characters. While we put individual letters together to form words, a single Chinese character may be used to represent a whole word.

2. Invite students to learn more about Chinese writing by clicking on the links at the above Web site. They can read about the origins of Chinese writing and how it developed from simple pictographs (picture words) to intricate characters.

3. Photocopy and distribute page 31 to each student. As they begin to draw their characters, have them think about the origins of Chinese writing.

More To Do:

Fun With Fonts

Whether written in print, manuscript, or calligraphy, we can easily recognize an A or any other letter of our alphabet. Encourage students to explore various ways we represent letters—one way is to experiment with fonts (typefaces) on the computer. Next time they need to write a paper or create a display, have students try out different fonts. You may want to point out that some fonts are harder to read than others. Explain that while a beautiful script may be attractive to the eye, people may have difficulty reading it.

Name(s) ____

GO TO: www.scholastic.com/profbooks/netexplorations/index.htm

Chinese Calligraphy

One sign of an advanced civilization is the people's ability to communicate through writing. Browse the links at the above Web site to learn about the history of writing in China. Below are some Chinese characters and their definitions. Try to redraw the characters in the second column. In the third column, use your imagination to create your own characters for the same words.

Chinese characters		Draw the Chinese characters here	Create your own characters for the same words here
Fire	火		
Child	子		
Heart	心		
Tree	木		
Mountain	山		

GO TO: www.scholastic.com/profbooks/netexplorations/index.htm

Social Studies

Greek Chronology

Students complete a time line of ancient Greece.

BACKGROUND

Ancient Greek civilization started around 2000 BC, when people from the north arrived in Greece and established small farming villages. Over the centuries, different groups of people including Minoans, Mycenaeans, and Dorians controlled the region. Greece's Golden Age began around 477 BC, when Greece produced its best artistic and literary work. As their culture advanced and transformed, the Greeks continued to dominate the western world for centuries.

DOING THE ACTIVITY

1. Ask students, What is a time line? *(A type of chart that chronologically lists the most important events in history)* Tell students that they will be creating a time line of ancient Greece, focusing on events that took place from the time of Mycenaean domination until the Roman conquest.

2. Photocopy and distribute page 33 to each student pair or small group. Have students look at the different years for which they'll need to find information.

3. Invite students to browse the links at the above Web site to read about ancient Greece. As they come across the relevant dates, have them make notes on the chart provided.

ANSWERS

146 BC: Greece is conquered by the Romans; **336 BC:** Alexander the Great's reign begins; **338 BC:** Philip II of Macedonia conquers the Greeks; **431 BC:** The Peloponnesian Wars begin; **479 and 490 BC:** The Greeks defeat invading Persian armies; **776 BC:** The first Olympic Games; **1200 BC:** The Trojan War and the fall of the Myceneans; **2000 BC:** Mycenaean culture inhabits Greek mainland; **3000 BC:** Minoan culture inhabits the island of Crete.

More To Do:

Ancient Greece's Contributions

During their Golden Age, the ancient Greeks produced their best artistic and literary works. The ancient Greeks were also known for other great contributions to the modern world. For example, they founded the concept of democracy. Challenge students to research and report on other contributions that the Greeks made.

Name(s) ______________________________

GO TO: www.scholastic.com/profbooks/netexplorations/index.htm

Time Line: Ancient Greece

Explore the links at the above Web site to learn about the history of ancient Greece. Look at the dates listed in the time line below. List the major events that made each of these dates significant.

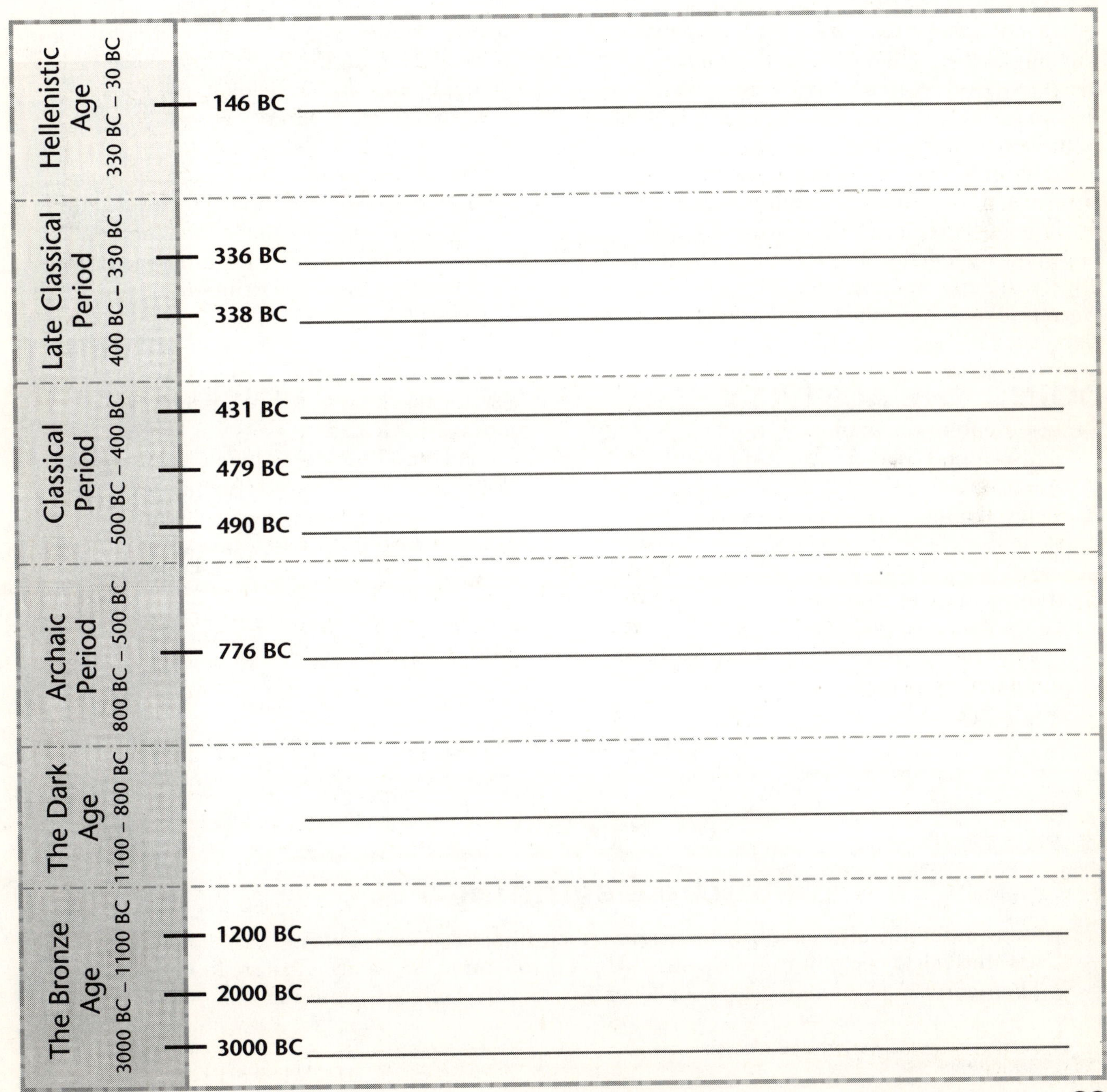

GO TO: www.scholastic.com/profbooks/netexplorations/index.htm

Greek Gods and Goddesses

Students create a family tree of the Greek gods and goddesses.

BACKGROUND

In ancient times people used myths to explain why things such as lightning and thunder occurred. Gods played a huge role in mythology, and each had his or her own specific area of influence. For example, the Greek god Zeus, in addition to being the king of the gods, was also the god of lightning and thunder. In Greek mythology, there are 12 Olympian gods (six male and six female) who ruled from Mount Olympus: Zeus, Apollo, Ares, Hephaestus, Hermes, Poseidon, Athena, Aphrodite, Artemis, Demeter, Hera, and Hestia.

DOING THE ACTIVITY

1. List the following names on the board: Zeus, Hera, Poseidon, Ares, Aphrodite, and Athena. Ask students if any of the names sound familiar and what they know about them.

2. Inform students that these names belong to Greek gods and goddesses. Explain that the ancient Greeks often made offerings to these deities, who they believed watched over them.

3. Invite students to learn more about the gods by clicking on the links at the above Web site. Point out that many of the gods are related to each other.

4. Photocopy and distribute page 35 to each student pair or small group. Have students create a family tree that shows the relationship between each god. Under each god's name, have students write what he or she is known for.

ANSWERS

Answers may vary, but could include the following information: Zeus was brother to Hestia, Hera, Poseidon, Hades, and Demeter. With Hera, Zeus fathered Athena, Ares, Hebe, and Hephaestus. With Leto, Zeus fathered Apollo and Artemis. With Maia, Zeus fathered Hermes, and with Dione, Zeus fathered Aphrodite.

More To Do:

In the Beginning . . .

Many different cultures and religions have their own "creation" stories—tales that explain how the world began. Invite students to do research and pick a particular creation story. Then encourage them to put on a play of the story they chose for the class.

Name(s) ____

GO TO: www.scholastic.com/profbooks/netexplorations/index.htm

Heavenly Family

Most of the Greek gods and goddesses were related to each other. Discover how by clicking on the links at the above Web site. Create a family tree of the gods and goddesses below. List children below their parents. Use a plus (+) sign between parents' names and put siblings next to each other on the same line. Write what each god is known for beneath his or her name.

Zeus
King of the Gods

GO TO: www.scholastic.com/profbooks/netexplorations/index.htm

Social Studies
Critical Thinking

Famous Romans

Students try to identify famous Romans by reading first-person monologues.

BACKGROUND

Rome was initially ruled by kings. When the last king, Tarquin, was overthrown in 510 BC, Rome became a republic for the next 400 years. The republic was ruled by the Senate, or officials elected to office by select Romans. In the 1st century BC, army generals ruled. But with the expansion of the Roman empire, there were too many conflicts between leaders. It was then decided around 27 BC that one man, Augustus, would rule. The emperors that ruled Rome were all quite different from one another. Some were kind, generous, and responsible for great advancements, while others were tyrannical.

DOING THE ACTIVITY

1. Ask students to name some famous Romans and what they know about them. Some may be familiar with Julius Caesar, Mark Antony, or Nero. Explain that these people ruled (or tried to rule) Rome at some point in time. Some of these rulers expanded the Roman empire and did great things, while others were tyrannical and made life difficult for the people.

2. Photocopy and distribute page 37 to each student. Together with the class, read each of the monologues on the page.

3. Challenge students to identify the rulers described by browsing the links at the above Web site. Have students write their answers on the page.

ANSWERS

1. Claudius; **2.** Caesar; **3.** Antony; **4.** Augustus; **5.** Nero; **6.** Titus

More To Do:

I Am Roman

Invite students to pick a famous Roman who is not included on the worksheet. Challenge them to write a monologue that the Roman may use to describe himself.

Name(s) ____

GO TO: www.scholastic.com/profbooks/netexplorations/index.htm

Famous Romans

The Romans described below were famous (or infamous) for different reasons. Read the monologues below, then try to identify the person. Click on the links at the above Web site to help you. Hint: These were emperors or politicians who lived between 100 BC-100 AD.

1. When my crazy nephew Caligula was murdered, I became emperor of Rome. I helped improve the judicial system, built cities and ports, and developed a safe way to import grain. But lucky in love? No way! My first wife conspired against me, and my second wife poisoned me. I AM ______________________________.

2. As a general, politician, and statesman, I was one of the most influential Romans of all time. My victory in Gaul further expanded the Roman Empire. Eventually I became dictator of all Rome. But I should have stayed home on March 15th. Et tú, Bruté? I AM ______________________________.

3. Caesar put me in charge of Italy. After his assassination, Caesar's adopted son became my biggest rival. I married his sister, Octavia, but my true love was Cleopatra, the queen of Egypt. When Octavia and I divorced, her brother declared war on me. Cleopatra and I joined forces, but we lost.
I AM ______________________________.

4. My great uncle, Julius Caesar, adopted me. I won the war against Antony in Actium and forced him to flee. I also built many roads, buildings, and aqueducts. Quite impressive for the first emperor of Rome.
I AM ______________________________.

5. I was only 17 when I became emperor. Even though my mother Agrippina helped get me the job, I had her executed. I loved music and poetry and forced the Roman people to watch me perform. When Rome burned, I blamed the Christians. Ignore those rumors about me starting the fire!
I AM ______________________________.

6. When I captured Jerusalem in 70 AD, my father, Vespasian, put me in command of the Praetorian Guard. I was very popular because I helped rebuild Campania after Vesuvius erupted, and Rome after the great fire. Not too bad, considering I only served 26 months in office! I AM ______________________________.

GO TO: www.scholastic.com/profbooks/netexplorations/index.htm

Social Studies
Language Arts

Daily Life in Ancient Rome

Students write the diary entry of a day in the life of an ancient Roman citizen.

BACKGROUND

From the beginning of the work day to the evening entertainment, daily life in Roman times was a fairly regulated regime. One's social standing depended on a variety of things, such as gender, education, land ownership, material belongings, or marital status. City life was considered the only civilized existence. How Romans personally conducted themselves in daily life was a reflection on their society as a whole.

DOING THE ACTIVITY

1. Ask students what they think people in ancient civilizations, like ancient Rome, might have been like. In what ways were these people similar to us? In what ways were they different?

2. Have students click on the links at the above Web site to help them understand the daily aspects of life in ancient Rome.

3. Photocopy and distribute page 39 to each student. Ask students to write a diary entry describing their life as a Roman living about 2,000 years ago.

4. When finished, have your students share their diaries with the rest of the class. Ask students to explain why they chose to write from the perspective of that person in their diary.

More To Do:

Got Class?

Like other civilizations, ancient Rome had different social classes, including the *plebians* (lower class) and *patricians* (upper class). Each class has its own role in society. Divide the class into small groups and assign each group a social class to research. Then hold an "Ancient Rome Day," where students will role-play according to their social classes. Encourage students to dress, eat, work, and behave the way someone in their social class would have back in ancient Rome.

Name(s) ____

GO TO: www.scholastic.com/profbooks/netexplorations/index.htm

My Life as a Roman

What was it like to live in ancient Rome? Visit the links at the above Web site to help you understand daily life there. Then, using the prompts below, write about your life as an ancient Roman.

My name is ______________________________________ .

I am __________ years old. I am a male/female (circle one).

I live in ______________________________ with my family.

Members of my family include

____

____ .

At home, I like to ______________________________ .

I wear ______________________________________ .

My favorite food is ______________________________ .

For fun, I like to______________________________ .

My education consists of ___________________________

____ .

GO TO: www.scholastic.com/profbooks/netexplorations/index.htm

Social Studies
Science
Math
Art

The Mayan Calendar

Students complete a Mayan calendar and compare it to our modern-day calendar.

BACKGROUND

The Mayans were a group of Native American Indian tribes that flourished primarily in southern Mexico, Guatemala, and Belize from around 2000 BC to 1540 AD. This culture produced advanced mathematicians and astronomers who developed two kinds of calendars—a religious calendar called the *Tzolkin* with 260 days, and a civil calendar called the *Haab* with 365 days, based on the Earth's orbit around the sun. The Haab consisted of 18 months with 20 days each, plus five extra days at the end of the year. During these five "unlucky" days, the Mayans fasted, sacrificed, and avoided unnecessary work.

DOING THE ACTIVITY

1. Hold a discussion about our modern-day calendar. Ask, How many months are in one calendar year? *(12)* How many days are in a year? *(365)* Why do you think there are 365 days in one calendar year? *(It takes the Earth 365 days to orbit around the sun.)*

2. Explain to students that the calendar we use today was developed around the 1580s while the Mayan calendar, which is as accurate as our calendar today, was developed more than 2,000 years ago.

3. Photocopy and distribute page 41 to each student pair or small group. Tell students that they will reconstruct one of the months in a Mayan calendar.

4. Have students click on the links at the above Web site to learn more about the Mayan calendar. To complete their calendars, have students download and print the appropriate glyphs for the month and days. They can then cut and paste the glyphs on their calendars. They can also choose to draw the glyphs themselves.

ANSWERS

Month choices will vary. Days are in the following order: **1.** Imix; **2.** Ik; **3.** Akbal; **4.** Kan; **5.** Chicchen; **6.** Cimi; **7.** Manik; **8.** Lamat; **9.** Muluc; **10.** Oc; **11.** Chuen; **12.** Eb; **13.** Ben; **14.** Ix; **15.** Men; **16.** Cib; **17.** Caban; **18.** Etznab; **19.** Cauac; **0.** Ahau

More To Do:

Ancient Scientists

Modern-day scientists are amazed at how advanced ancient Mayans were when it came to mathematics and astronomy. Challenge students to do further research and find evidence of Mayan ingenuity. What relics or ruins prove that Mayans knew a lot about mathematics and astronomy?

Name(s) ______________________________

GO TO: www.scholastic.com/profbooks/netexplorations/index.htm

The Haab

Click on the links at the above Web site to view and learn more about the Mayan calendar. Then, download and print the glyph for the Mayan month you want to do, as well as the glyphs for the days of the month. Cut and paste them in the calendar below. (You can also draw the glyphs yourself.)

Month: ________________ Glyph: ________________

1	2	3	4	5
6	7	8	9	10
11	12	13	14	15
16	17	18	19	0

GO TO: www.scholastic.com/profbooks/netexplorations/index.htm

Social Studies
Language Arts

Chichén Itzá

Students create the Chichén Itzá Times, a newspaper featuring Mayan life in the city of Chichén Itzá.

BACKGROUND

The famous city of Chichén Itzá was a large cultural and ceremonial center, founded by the Maya-Itzáe who came to the Yucatan around 435–455 AD. The city was occupied twice—first around 495–690 AD, then again around 950–1200 AD. The city of Chichén Itzá featured outstanding architecture including pyramids, temples, ball courts, observatories, and sacrificial sites. Chichén Itzá is one of the most complete and impressive ancient Mayan sites still standing today.

DOING THE ACTIVITY

1. Inform students that Chichén Itzá was one of the most powerful Mayan cities. Like modern-day cities, Chichén Itzá was always bustling with many activities.

2. Divide students into small groups. Photocopy and distribute page 43 to each student group.

3. Tell students that each group will work as an editorial team from the Chichén Itzá *Times*. Each member of the group will be assigned one or two newspaper articles to research and write.

4. Have students click on the links at the above Web site to help them with the research and reporting. When students have finished their articles, have each group create a layout of the newspaper on separate pieces of paper. They can cut out the headlines on the student page and paste them along with their articles in their newspaper. They can also download and print photos from the Web sites. Make sure students provide proper credits for photos used.

More To Do:

Great Pyramids

Create a bulletin board display comparing the pyramids of ancient Mexico with the pyramids of ancient Egypt. What do they look like? What were they used for? How are they alike? How are they different?

Name(s) ____

GO TO: www.scholastic.com/profbooks/netexplorations/index.htm

The Chichén Itzá Times

Create your own newspaper about Mayan life in the city of Chichén Itzá. Below are some headlines that will provide you with ideas for articles in your newspaper. Cut out the headlines and use them in your version of the Chichén Itzá Times. Use the links at the above Web site to help with your research.

Getting Around Chichén Itzá	Time Out at the Ball Court
Equinox Extravaganza at Kukulcán!	It's in the Stars: Your Daily Horoscope from the Observatory
The Temple of Warriors: Take Two Serpents and Column Me in the Morning	Get Thee to the Nunnery!
What's Happening at the Cenoté?	Tzompantli: How to Get Those Stubborn Skeletons Out of Your Closet!

GO TO: www.scholastic.com/profbooks/netexplorations/index.htm

The Aztec Religion

Students complete a chart identifying the role of religion in various aspects of Aztec life.

BACKGROUND

The Aztec people ruled a large empire in central and southern Mexico from the 14th to the 16th century. Religion was the central focus of their civilization, with a different deity governing each aspect of life. They honored their gods by constructing large pyramid temples, making sculptures, and holding elaborate ceremonies that involved human sacrifice. One of the two Aztec calendars was created exclusively for religious purposes.

DOING THE ACTIVITY

1. Explain to students that for the Aztecs, religion was not just a single part of their life—it was the very core of their existence. Ask, How does this compare with the way religion is practiced in our society today?

2. Photocopy and distribute page 45 to each student pair or small group.

3. Invite students to visit the links at the above Web site to learn more about the Aztec religion and its influence on their daily lives. Have students fill in the chart.

4. When they're finished, invite students to share their answers with the class. Compile all their answers on a single, large chart.

ANSWERS

Area	Religion's Influence	Gods Associated With This Area
Agriculture	Worshipped gods of natural forces to ensure good crops	Tlaloc, Itzpzpalotl, Centeotl, Chalchiuhtlicue, Mayahuel, Quilaztli, Tonacateuctli
Architecture	Temples built for religious ceremonies	
Art	Primarily created for depiction of the gods	
Astronomy	One of two calendars used solely for religious purposes	Metztli, Chiuateteo, Cipactonal, Citlalatonac, Tecciztecatl
Medicine	Disease was the will of the gods. Used spiritual and herbal healing to cure symptoms.	Patecatll
Music and Dance	Performed for the enjoyment of the gods	Macuilxochitl, Xochipilli, Ppilimtec
Sacrifice	Human sacrifice to appease the gods	Mictlantecuhtle, Chalmeccacihuatl
Warfare	Provided prisoners of war for sacrificial ceremonies	Tezcatlipoca, Huitzilopochtli

More To Do:

Aztec Basketball

Some Aztec ceremonial halls include a playing court for a game that resembles basketball. Invite students to research this ancient Aztec game and find out what role, if any, it played in the Aztec religion. Then have them compare the game to modern-day basketball. How are the games similar? How are they different?

Name(s) ____

GO TO: www.scholastic.com/profbooks/netexplorations/index.htm

Gods of the Aztec

Religion played a major role in Aztec society. Visit the links at the above Web site to help you complete the chart below. In the second column, describe how religion influenced each aspect of their society. In the last column, name the Aztec gods who are associated with that area. (Some areas may be influenced by more than one god, while others may have none at all.)

Area	Religion's Influence	Gods Associated With This Area
Agriculture		
Architecture		
Art		
Astronomy		
Medicine		
Music and Dance		
Sacrifice		
Warfare		

GO TO: www.scholastic.com/profbooks/netexplorations/index.htm

Social Studies
Critical Thinking

End of the Aztec Empire

Students complete a cause-and-effect chart that explains the downfall of the Aztec Empire.

BACKGROUND

The Aztecs (1100–1522 AD) were considered the last of the great ancient civilizations. In 1519, Hernán Cortés, a Spanish conquistador, left Cuba for Mexico. In Mexico, he amassed the support of 150,000 native people who were hostile to the Aztecs, along with 400 of his own troops, and began a series of attacks. When half of the population of Tenochtitlan died from smallpox, Cortés seized and destroyed this capital city of the Aztecs. By August 1521, the Aztec empire was completely wiped out and Spanish rule was declared.

DOING THE ACTIVITY

1. Inform students that around the 15th and 16th centuries, European explorers traveled far to learn more about the world. Ask, What often happened when these explorers encountered another civilization? *(The Europeans often conquered the other civilization.)* Explain that the Aztec civilization met its downfall when Spanish conquistador Hernán Cortés arrived in Mexico.

2. Photocopy and distribute page 47 to each student.

3. Invite students to review the links at the above Web site to learn the details about the conquest of the Aztecs by Hernán Cortés. Have students complete the cause-and-effect chart on the page.

4. When they're finished, hold a classroom discussion. Ask, What do you think the Aztecs could have done differently to avoid getting conquered?

More To Do:

City of Gold

El Dorado, the legendary city of gold, was sought after by many of the Spanish conquistadors who came to the Americas in the 16th century. Have students research El Dorado to learn how the legend may have started, and where the city may have been located.

Name(s) ______________________________________

GO TO: www.scholastic.com/profbooks/netexplorations/index.htm

End of the Aztec Empire

In 1521 AD, Spanish conquistador Hernán Cortés successfully seized and destroyed the Aztec city of Tenochtitlan, marking the end of the last great ancient civilization. Read more about its tragic end by clicking on the links at the above Web site. Then write how each of the events on the left column led to the downfall of the Aztecs.

Causes		Effects
Moctezuma believed that Cortés was the god Quetzalcoatl.	→	
Neighboring Indian tribes resented the Aztecs.	→	
Cortés and his people brought smallpox and other diseases with them.	→	
Moctezuma presented gold and other jewelry to Cortés and his people.	→	

Resources

Books, Software, Videos, and Web sites

Teacher Resources

Exploring Ancient Cities (2nd Edition) (Sumeria, 1996). Explores four ancient cities: Teotihuican, Pompeii, Petra, and the Bronze Age palaces of Crete.

Nova: Secrets of Lost Empires (PBS, 1997). Five one-hour Nova video field trips.

Ancient Civilizations for Children Video Series (Schlessinger, 1998). A 9-video box set recommended for grades 3–7.

The Penguin Encyclopedia of Classical Civilizations edited by Arthur Cotterell (Penguin, 1996). Excellent overall reference source.

Ancient Civilizations: 3000 BC-AD 500 by the Editors of Time-Life Books (Time Life, 1998).

Ancient Egypt: Background and Information, Activities, Projects, Literature Links, and Posters by Ruth Akamine Wassynger (Scholastic, 1997). A fun, informative activity book recommended for grades 4–8.

Mayas, Aztecs, Incas: Cooperative Learning Activities by Mary Strohl and Susan Schneck (Scholastic, 1995). Learning activities about a range of subjects in all three cultures, for grades 4–8.

Education Planet
http://www.educationplanet.com/search/History/World_History/Ancient Civilizations

The Ancient World Web
http://www.julen.net/ancient

Student Resources

My First Amazing History Explorer (DK Multimedia). To rescue a professor who is lost in history, players travel back in time to ancient Egypt, the Roman Empire, and more.

The Greeks: Crucible of Civilization (PBS Home Video, 2001). Follows Greek civilization from its beginnings in 500 BC to its downfall.

National Geographic Video: Mysteries of Egypt (National Geographic, 1999).

Ancient History Links
http://killeenroos.com/link/anchist.htm

Encyclopedia of Civilizations, Explorations & Conquest by Philip Wilkinson, Will Fowler, Simon Adams, John Farndon (Lorenz Books, 2000). Recommended for ages 9–12.

Cleopatra VII: Daughter of the Nile by Kristiana Gregory (Scholastic, 1999). Twelve year-old Cleopatra keeps a diary about events in her daily life.

The Legend of Mu Lan: A Heroine of Ancient China by Wei Chiang, Cheng-An Chiang (Victory Press, 1997). In war-torn China, a girl disguises herself as her brother and defends her homeland.

The Ides of April by Mary Ray (Bethlehem Books, 1999). A historical mystery taking place in ancient Rome.